Mia Rosenthal

a little bit every day

Gallery Joe, Philadelphia
February 7 – March 22, 2014

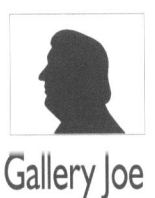

Gallery Joe

Front Gallery and Vault Gallery installation views

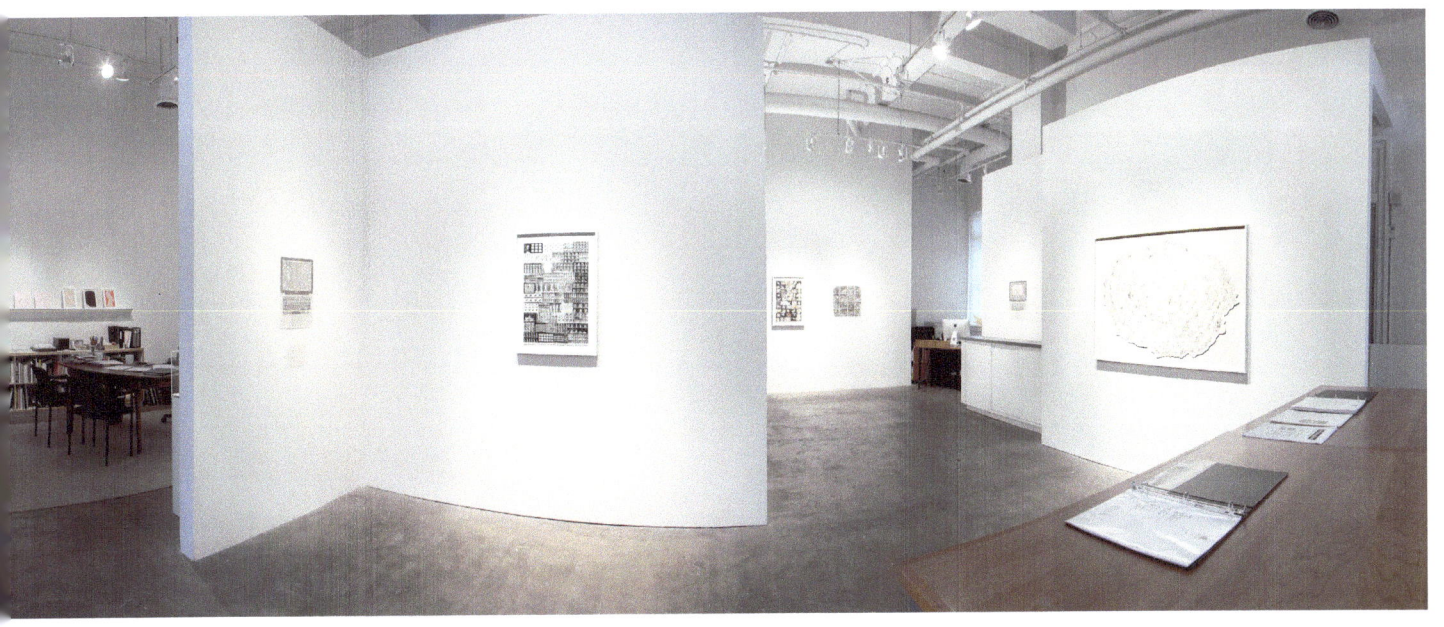

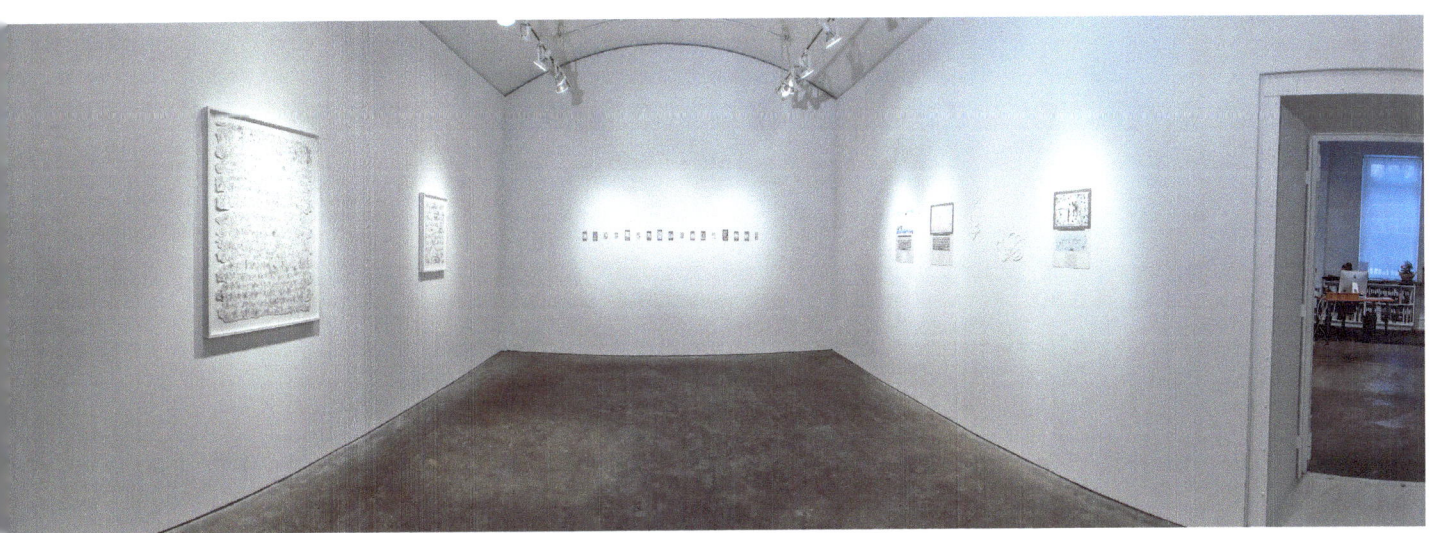

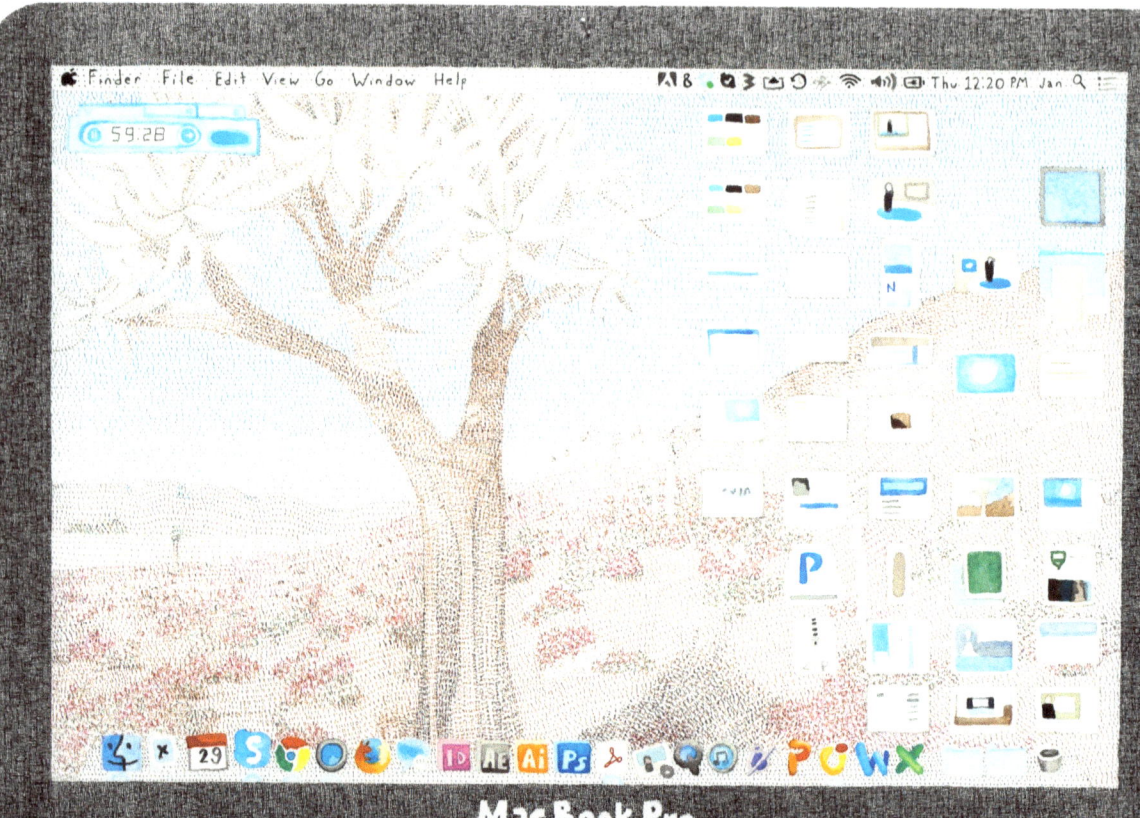

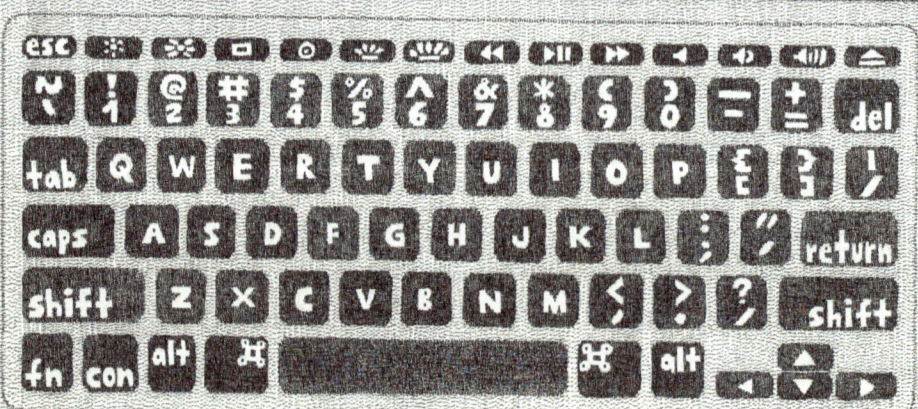

MacBook Pro

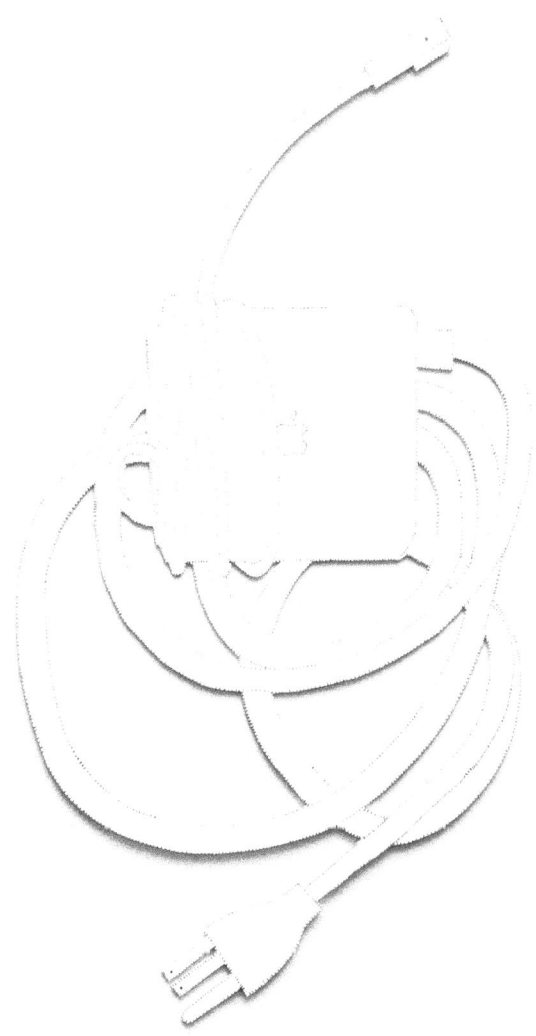

Drawing is one of the oldest activities in human history. Mia Rosenthal's large ambitious ink drawing: *Life on Earth*, spanning 38 x 55 inches, offers the rare opportunity for slow reflection on the history of the planet earth and its species – in particular, that of the human race. The drawing is akin to a spliced cross section of historical taxonomy in the form of a large spiral shaped drawing. The subject matter ranges from a single celled organism to a biogenetically engineered fruit fly (Drosophila synthetica, 2012).

Rosenthal's exhibition is a meta-reflection on the "every day", from her scaled drawings of mac i-phones to the large spiral-shaped *Life on Earth* drawing. What is fundamental about Rosenthal's work is how the drawn mark, like the spark of an idea of human imagination, drives this exhibition into motion. It's as if to suggest that the drawn mark takes on a life of its own and generates the entirety of the exhibition itself. In essence, the mark is absolutely fundamental in the artist's work – formally, individually, expansively, and conceptually.

Rosenthal's drawings utilize both form and inquiry – she is an artist whose practice is grounded in the idea as well as manipulating forms to discover the idea. Drawing from conceptual art she embraces the idea as the beginning of her art but finds value in the handcraft of art production itself. And because of the indifference of time, the artist can reflect on and reconsider the purist aspects of conceptual art, in which the earlier conceptualists in the 1960s and early 1970s challenged the value of traditional forms of art production by vanquishing the unique material form of aesthetic expression for the generic and the impersonal. Instead, Rosenthal sets out to re-engage the spectator with an "open inquiry" by presenting the spectator with her own practice, which incorporates both its avant-garde roots and traditional handcraft. Mia Rosenthal's *Life on Earth* is an affirmation of life itself, while also simultaneously emitting the symbol for entropy, reminding us that all things are subject to change. As a result, Rosenthal's exhibition offers the spectator multiple points of view ranging from the subject matter, to the construction of these drawings, and what they might mean in the larger context of aesthetic consideration.

– Todd Keyser

Life on Earth, 2013, 38 x 28 inches, ink on paper

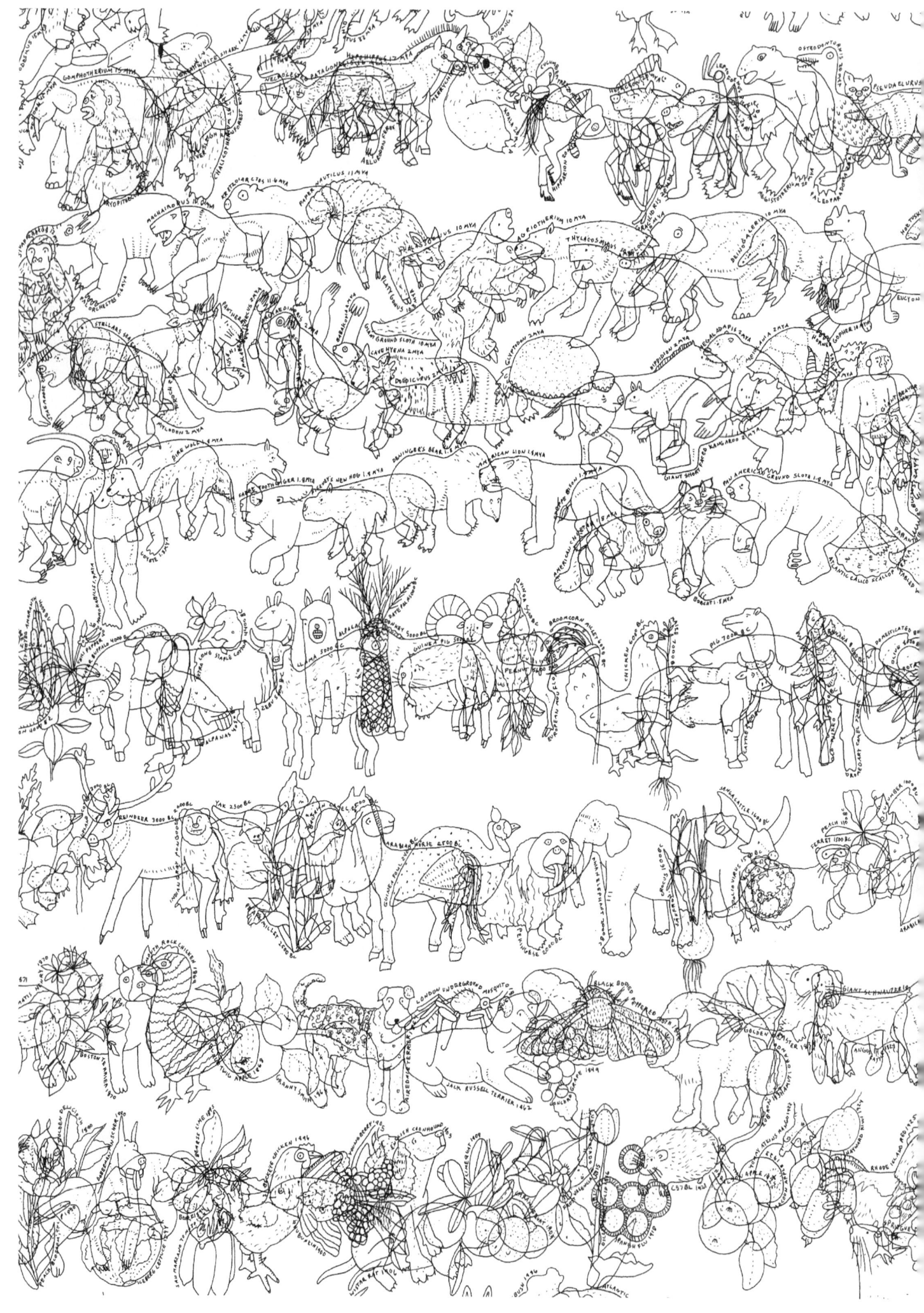

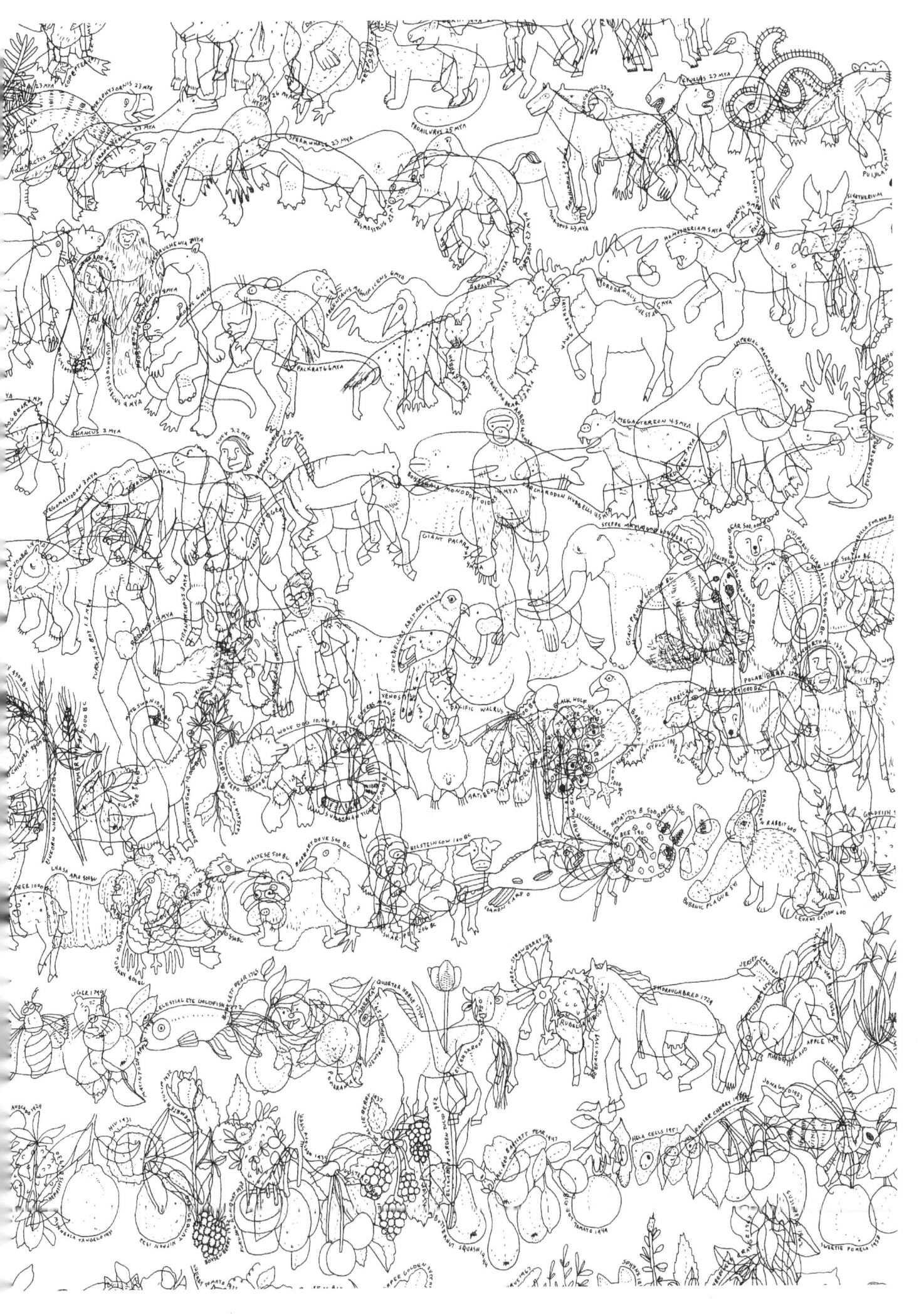

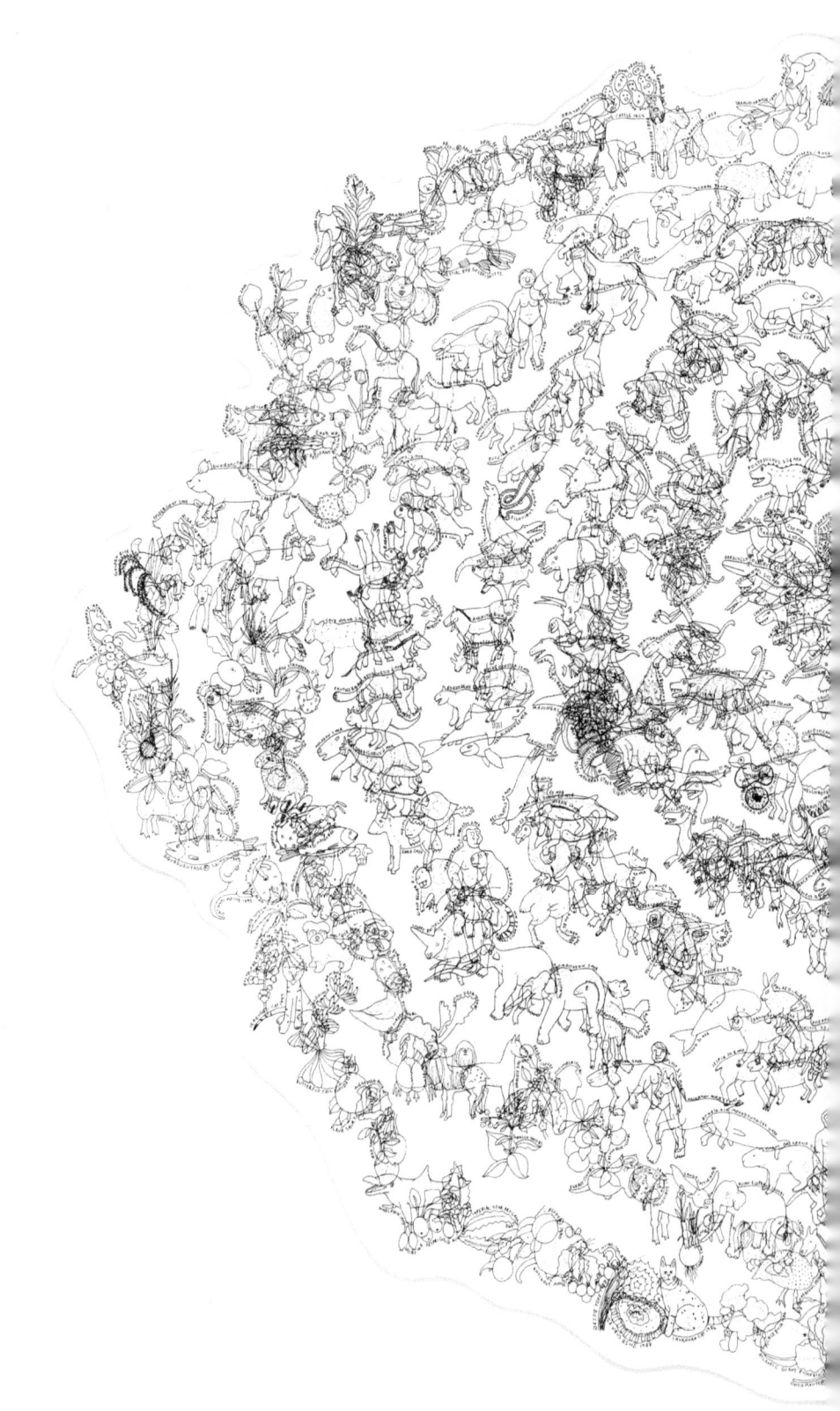

Life on Earth, 2013, 38 x 55 inches (irregular), ink on paper

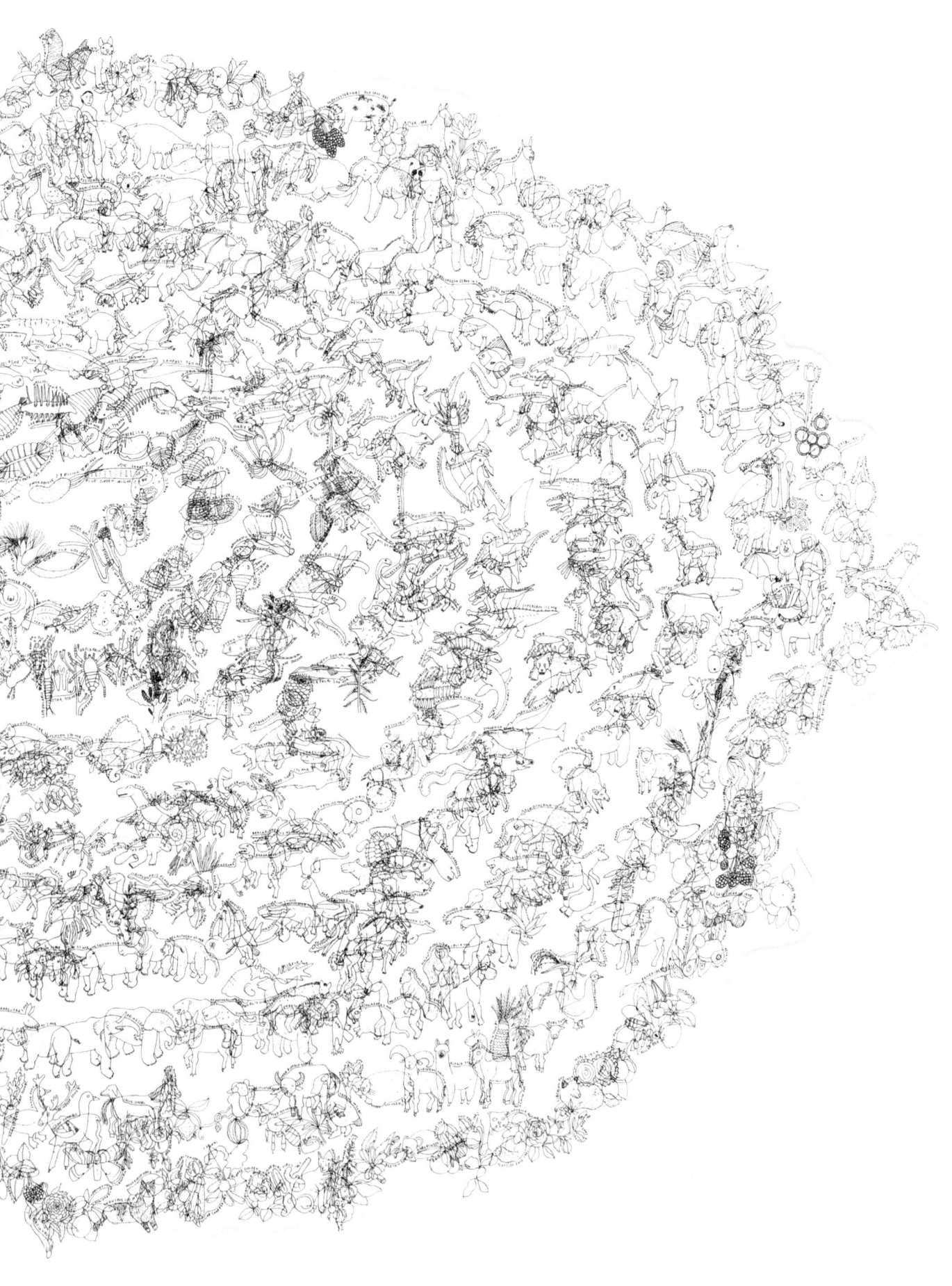

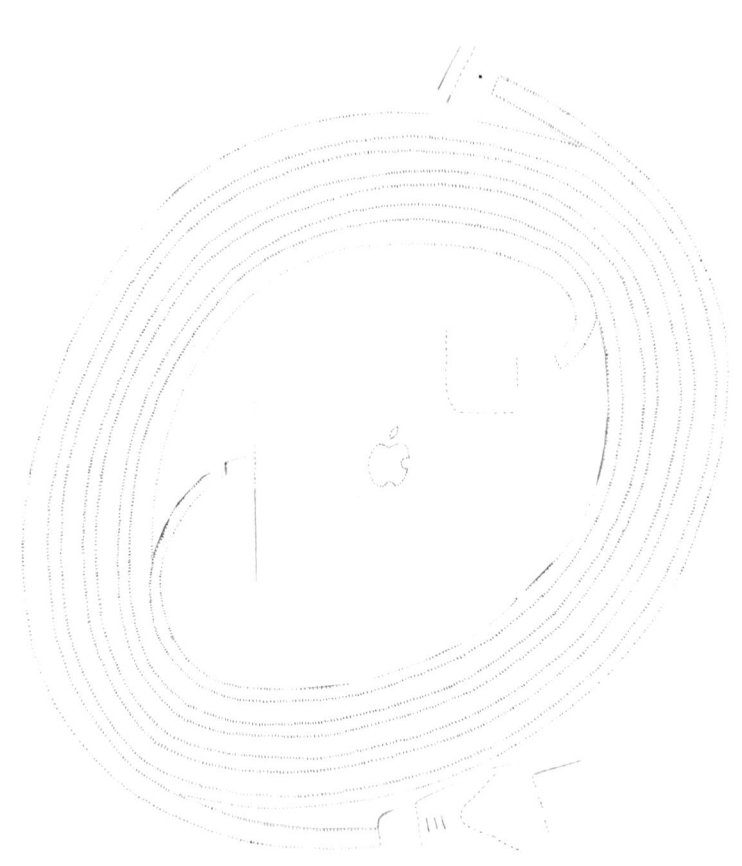

MacBook Pro (Scott), 2012, 19 ⅓ x 14 ⅓ and 8 ¾ x 8 inches, ink, gouache and graphite on paper

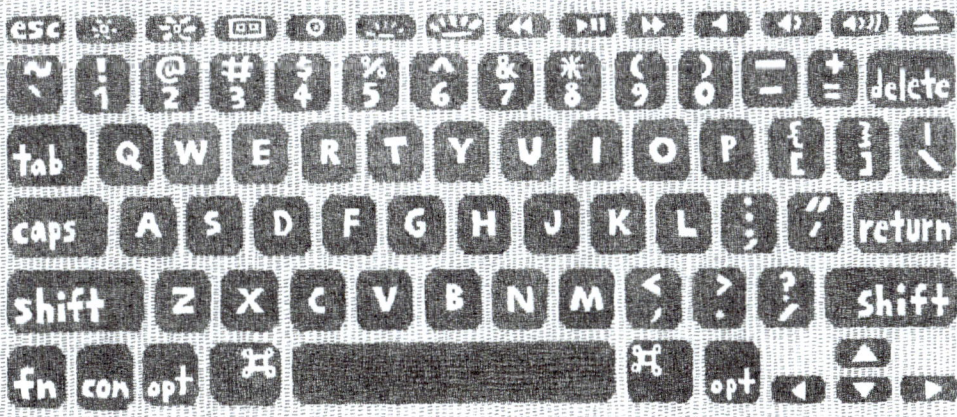

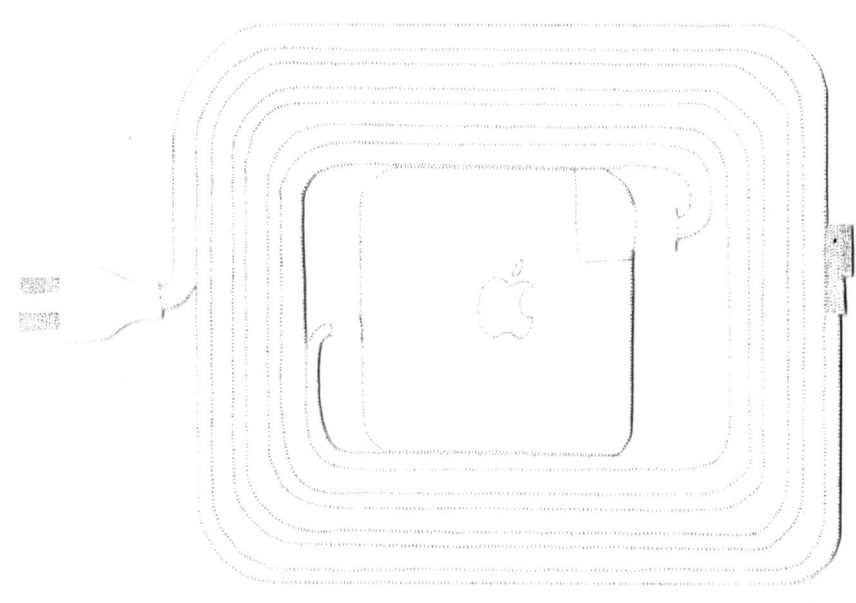

MacBook Pro (self portrait), 2012, 17 5/8 x 12 ½ and 5 3/8 x 8 3/8 inches, ink, gouache and graphite on paper

MacBook Pro

Francoluigi's Square Tomato Pie, 2014, 16 panels, each approximately 4½ x 4½ inches, ink on paper

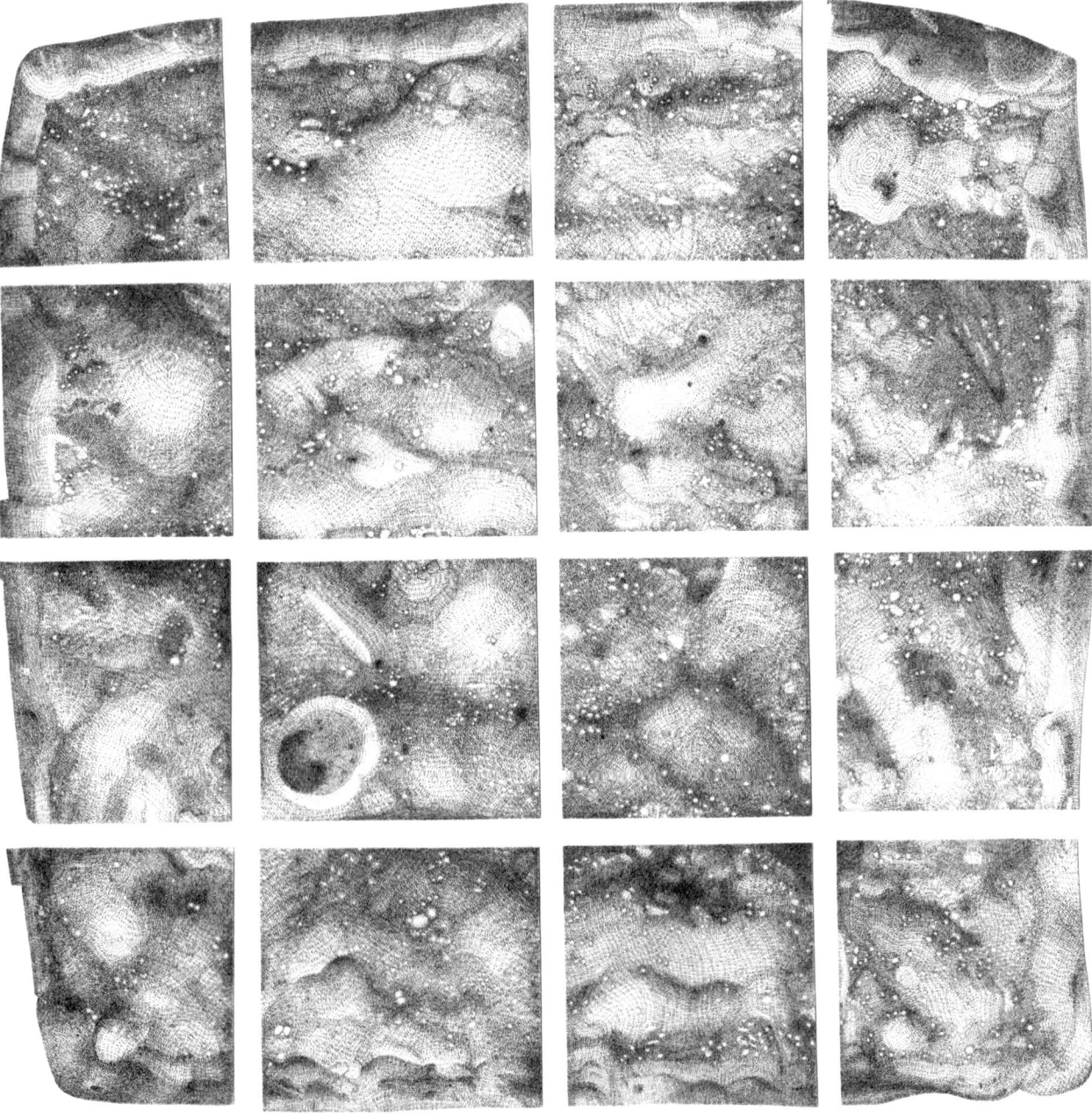

Google Portrait of Audubon, 2013, 22 x 15 inches, ink and pencil on paper

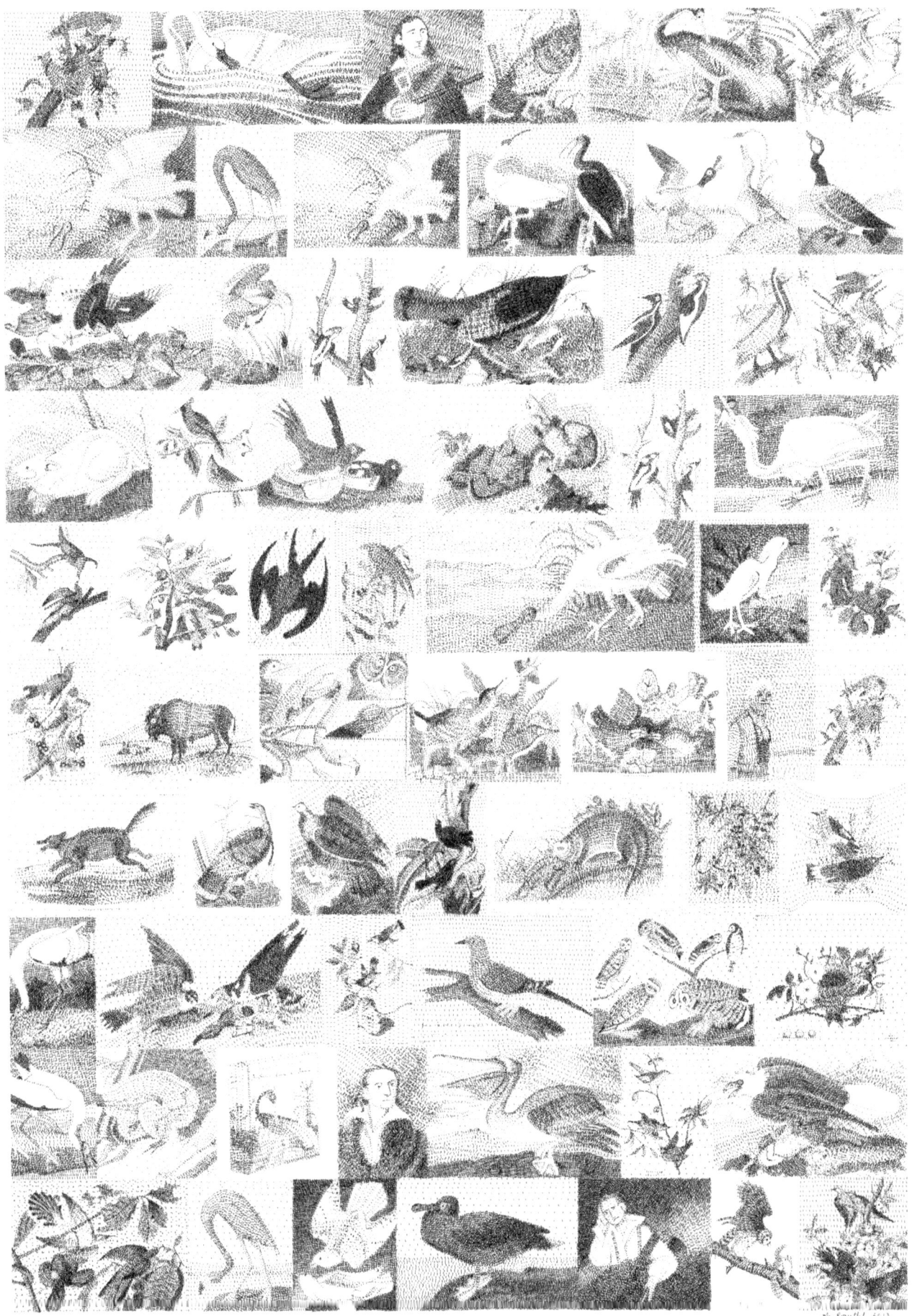

Google Portrait of Eadweard Muybridge, 2013, 26 x 17 inches, ink and pencil on paper

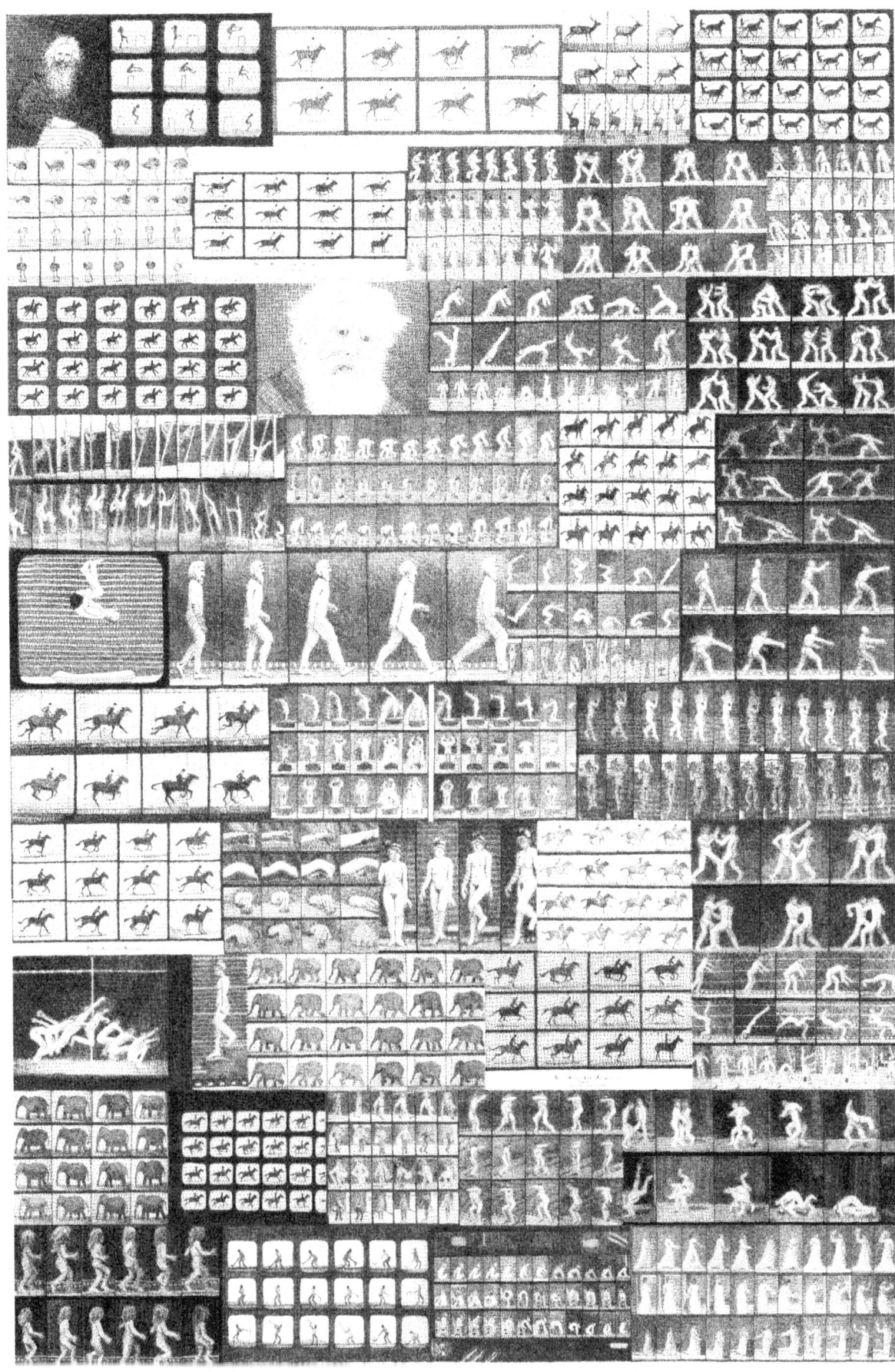

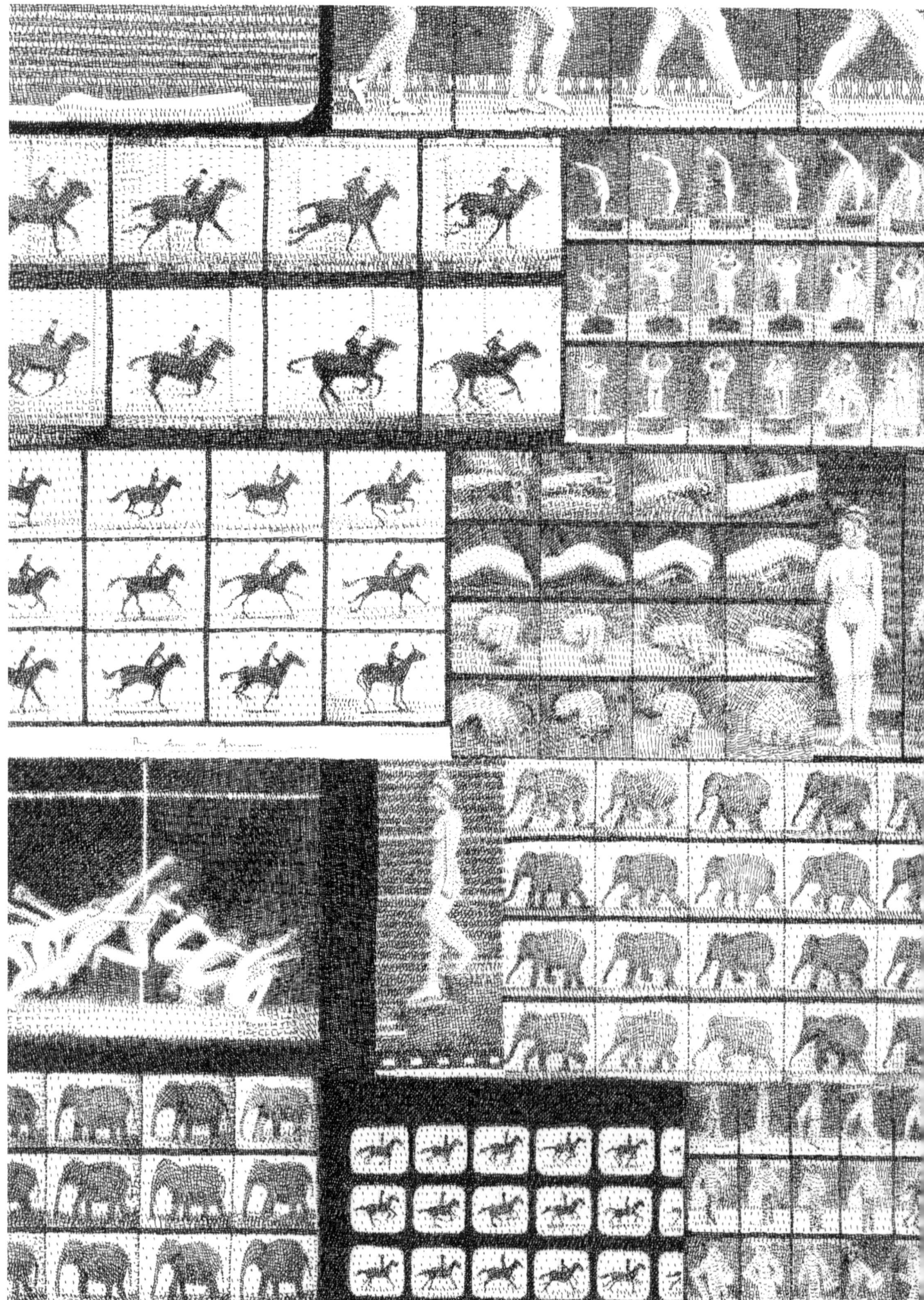

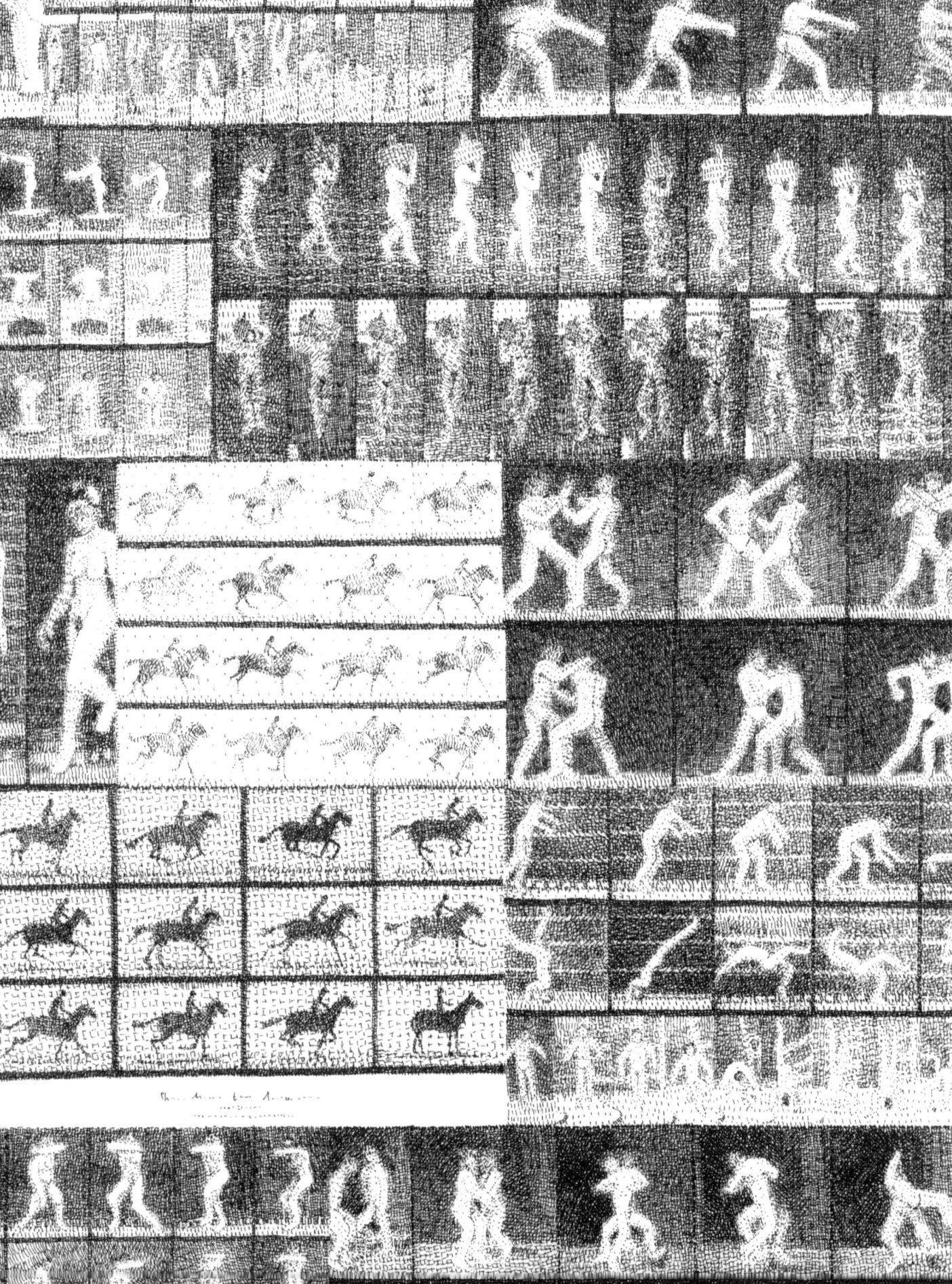

Google Portrait of Hubble Telescope, 2013, 26 ¼ x 17 inches, ink pencil and gouache on paper

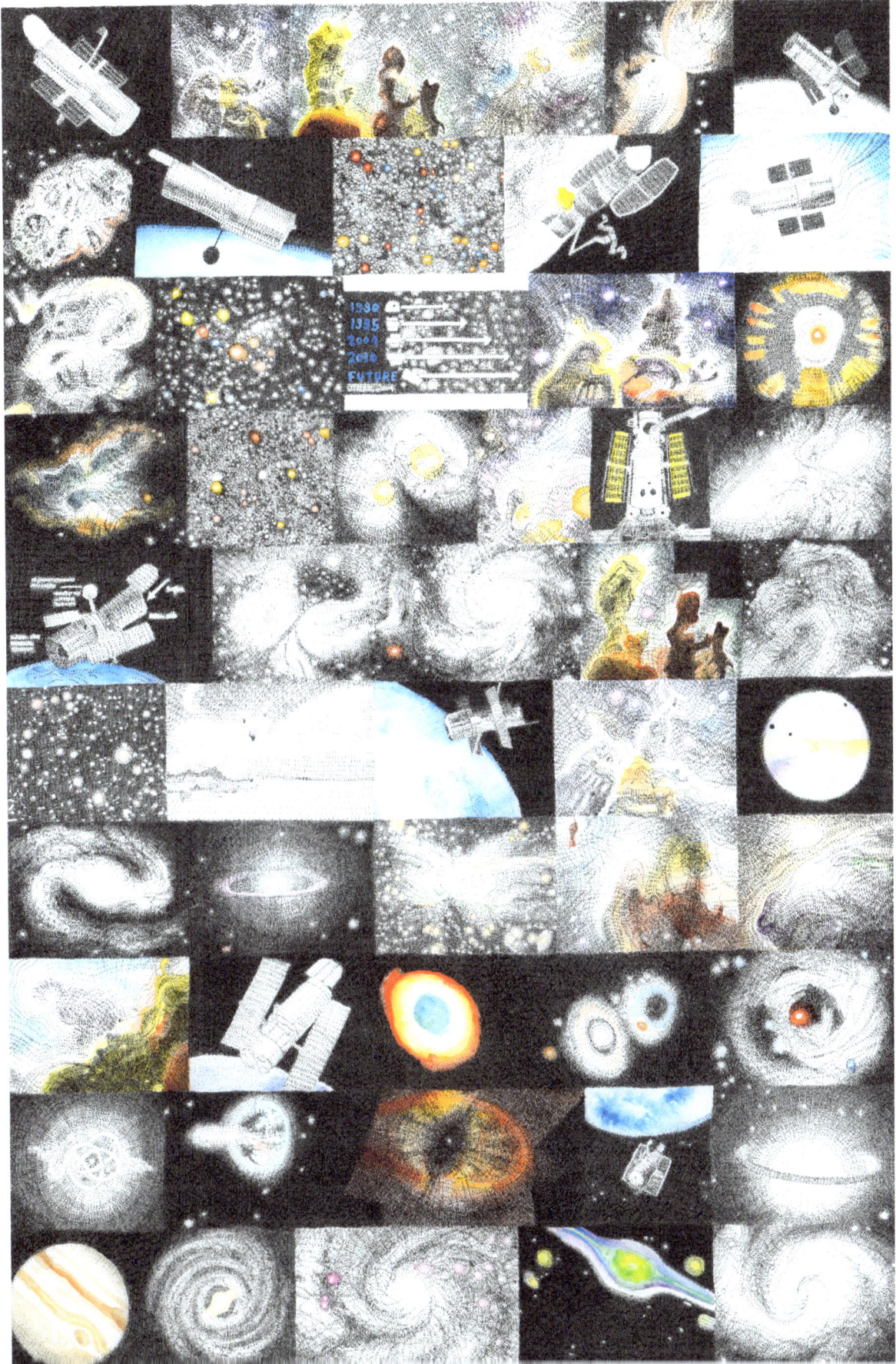

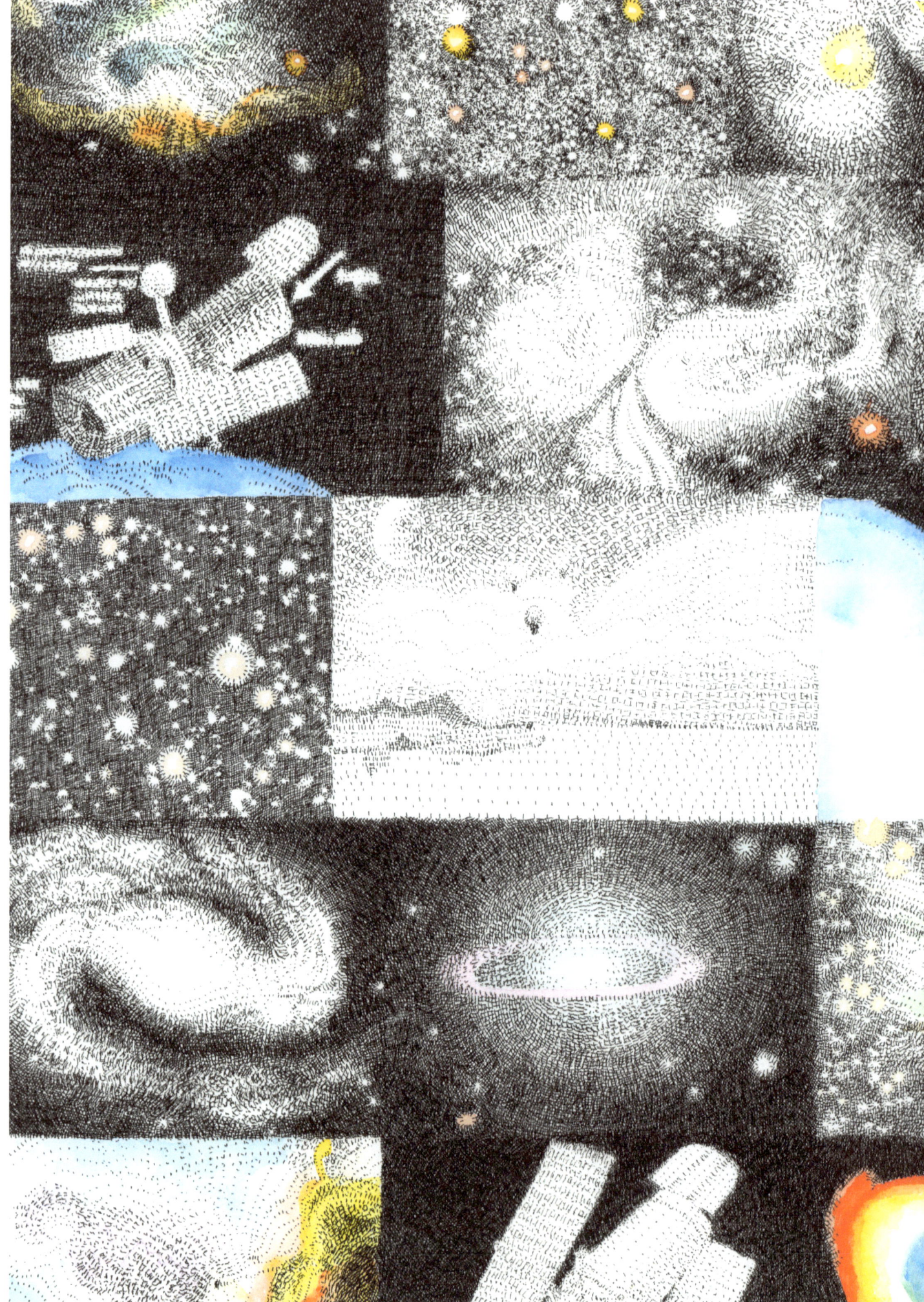

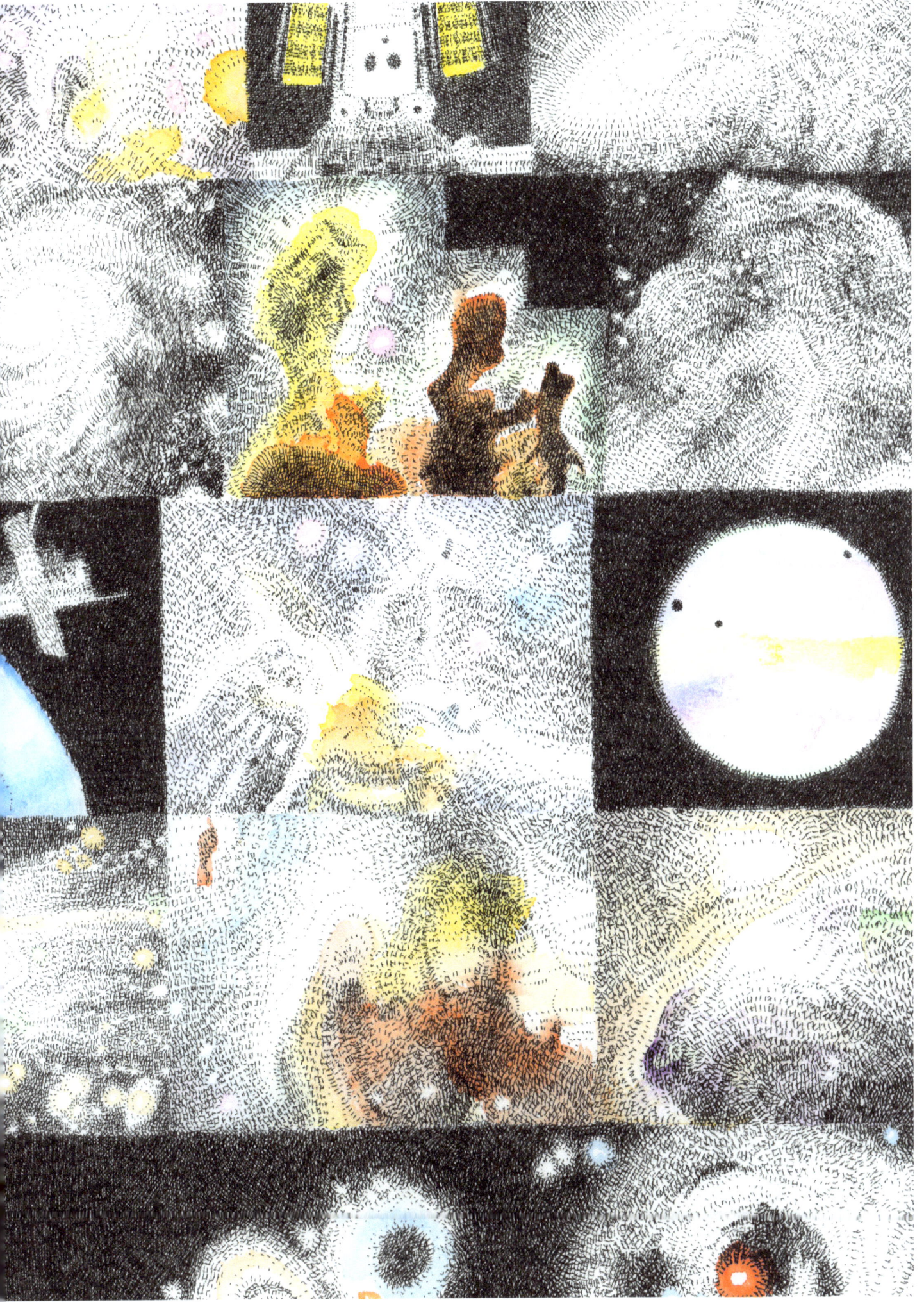

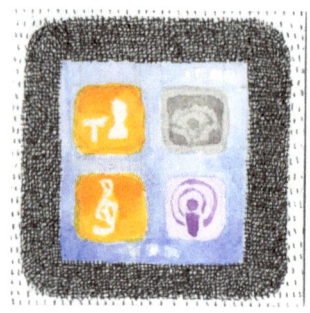

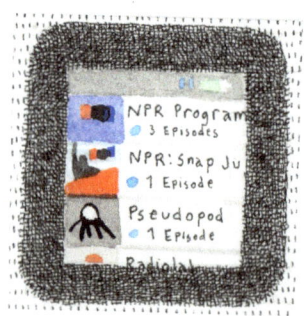

iPod Nano (Robert), 2014, 1½ x 1½ inches, ink, pencil and gouache on paper
iPod Nano (Robert), 2014, 1½ x 1½ inches, ink, pencil and gouache on paper
iPhone (Simona), 2014, 1½ x 1½ inches, 4 ½ x 2 ¼ inches, ink and pencil on paper
Motorola Droid Razr (Sam), 2014, 5 ¼ x 2 ¾ inches, ink, pencil and gouache on paper

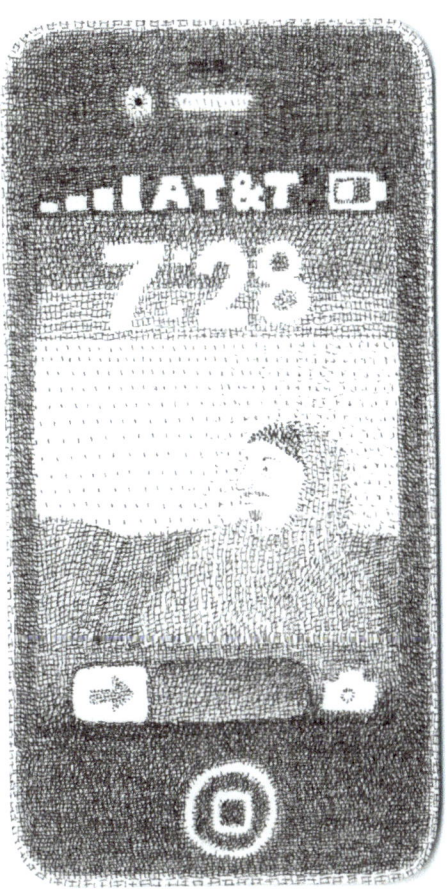

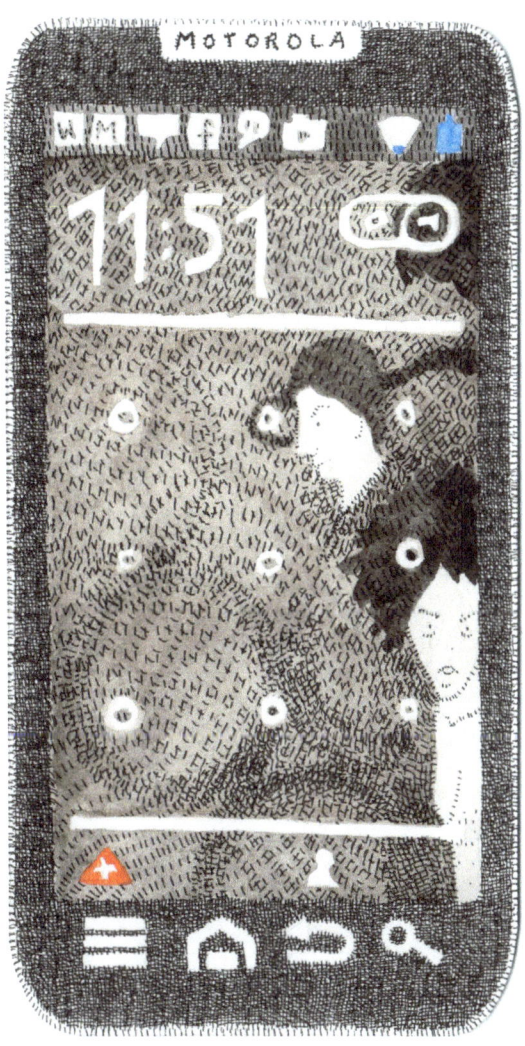

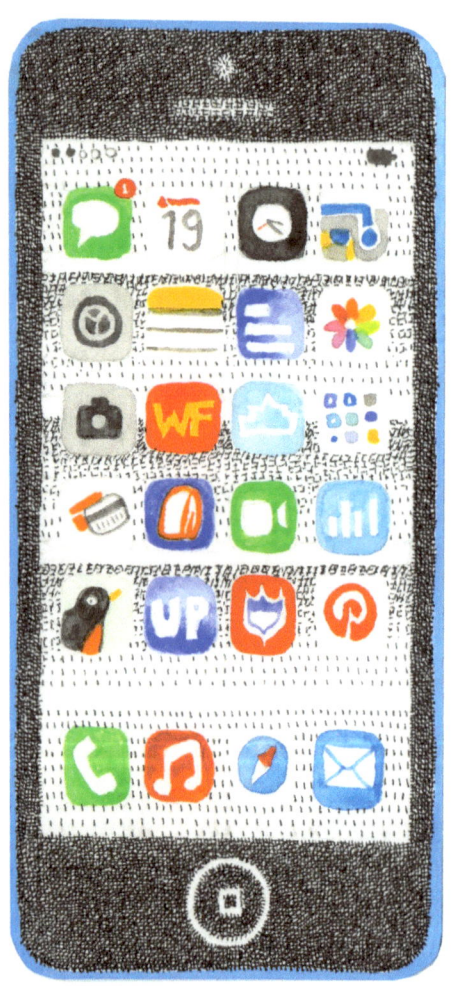
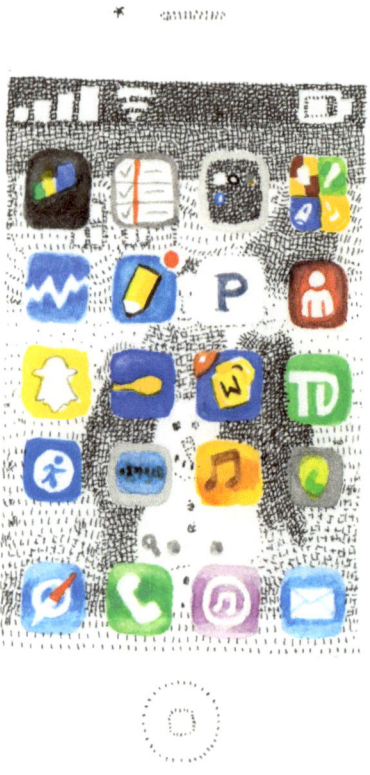

iPhone (Jay), 2014, 5 x 2 ¼ inches, ink, pencil and gouache on paper
iPhone (Loryn), 2014, 4 ½ x 2 ¼ inches, ink, pencil and gouache on paper
iPhone (Loryn), 2014, 4 ½ x 2 ¼ inches, ink and pencil on paper
Samsung Galaxy (Steve), 2014, 5 x 2 ½ inches, ink, pencil and gouache on paper

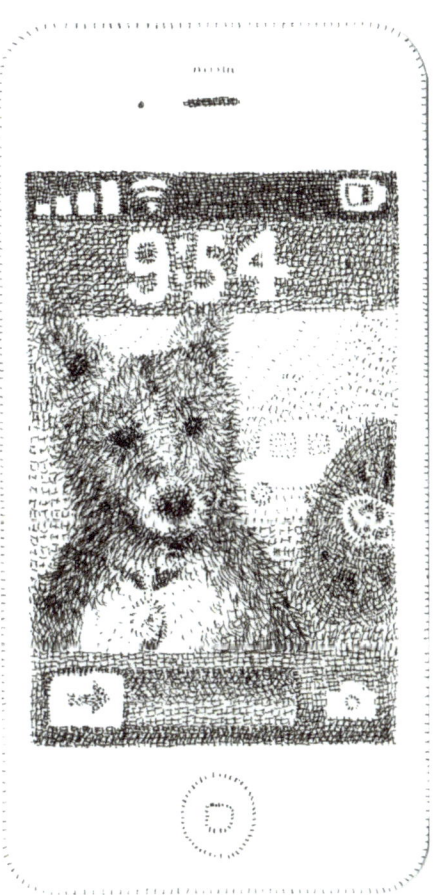
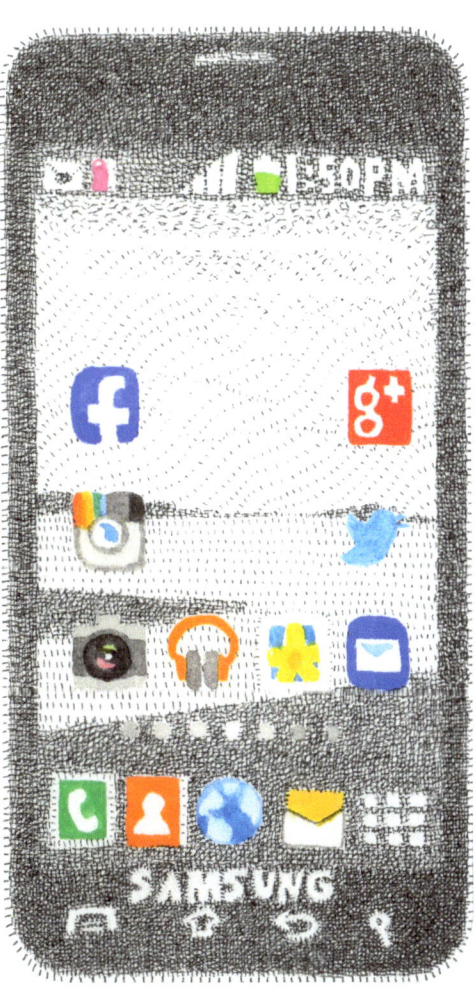

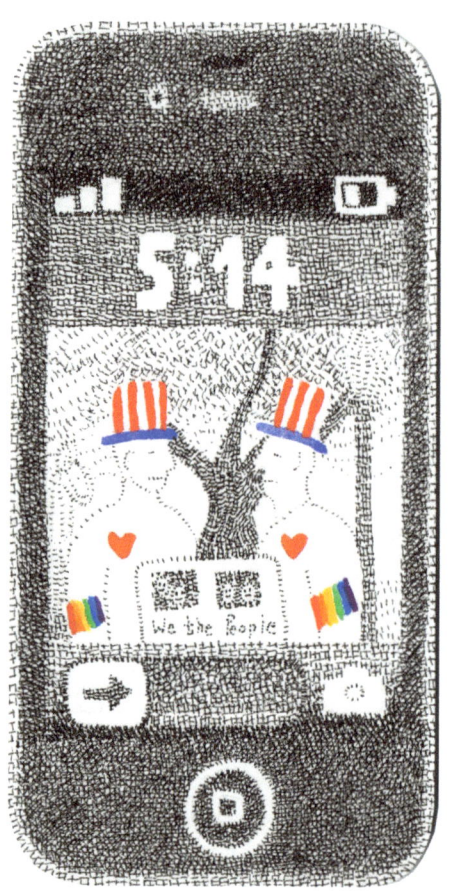 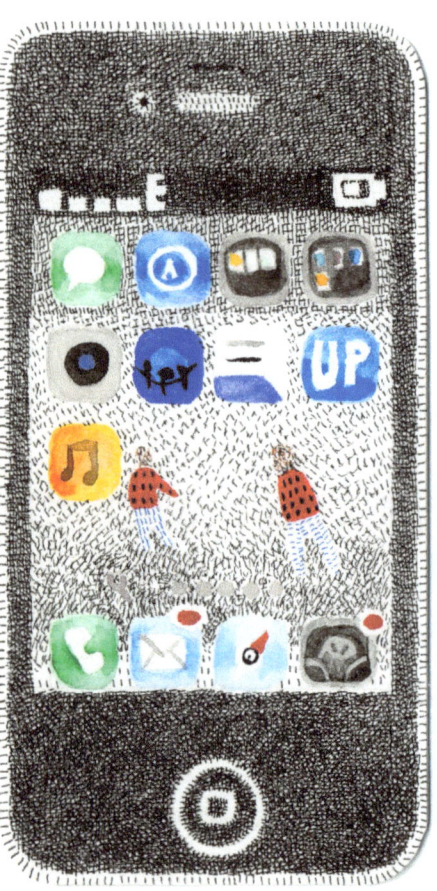

iPhone (Mark Sam), 2013, 4 ½ x 2 ¼ inches, ink, pencil and gouache on paper
iPhone (Kate), 2013, 4 ½ x 2 ¼ inches, ink, pencil and gouache on paper
iPhone (Hope), 2013, 4 ½ x 2 ¼ inches, ink, pencil and gouache on paper
iPhone (Rob), 2014, 4 ½ x 2 ¼ inches, ink, pencil and gouache on paper

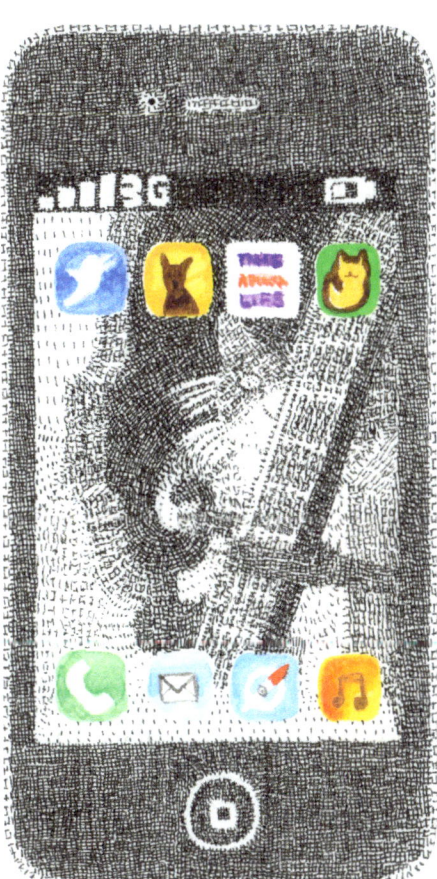
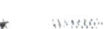

I Remember That Day, 2013, 11x 14 inches, ink on paper (handmade abaca by Alexis Granwell)

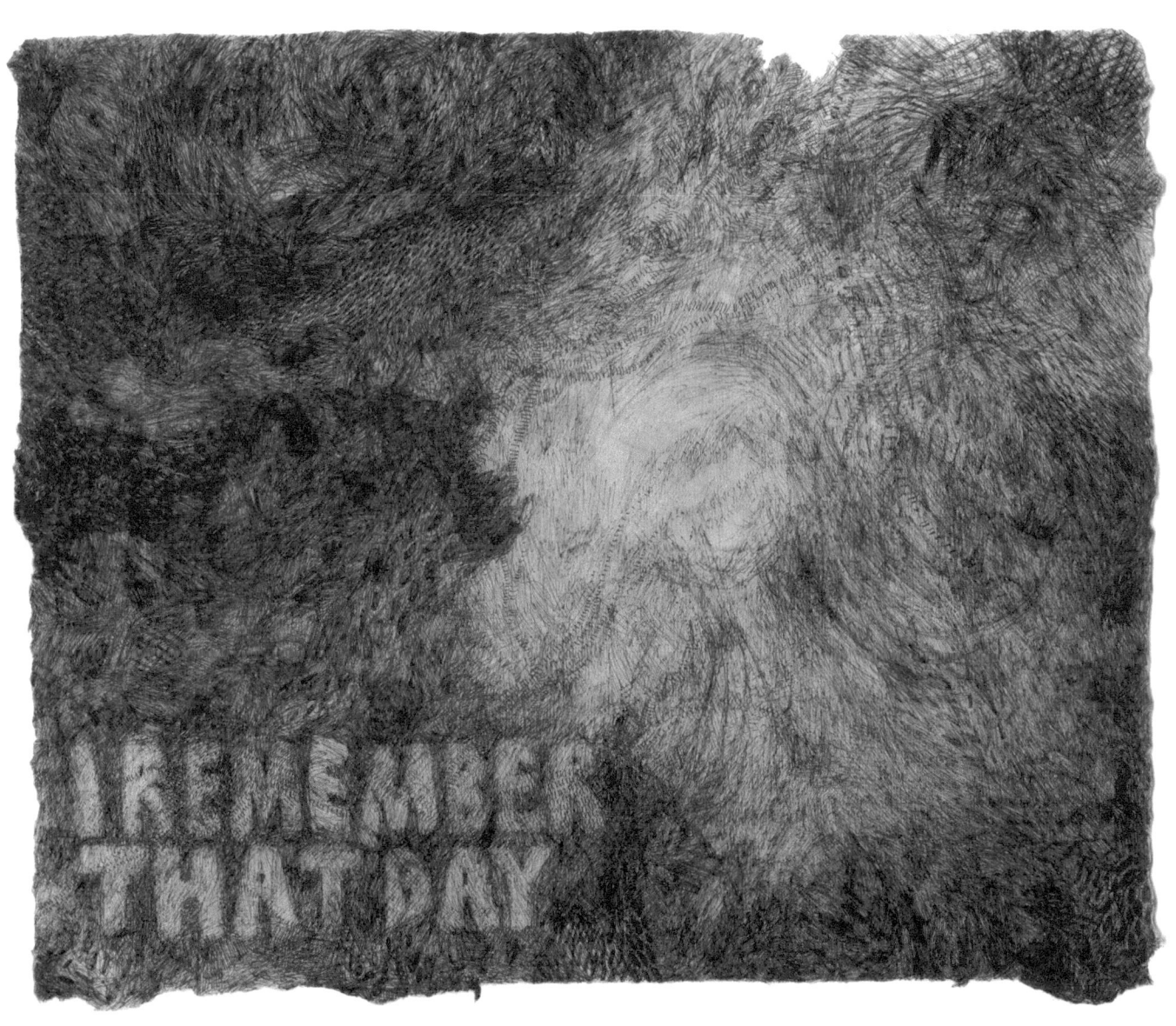

Mia Rosenthal: a little bit every day
February 7 – March 22, 2014

Gallery Joe
302 Arch Street, Philadelphia, PA 19106
215.592.7752
www.galleryjoe.com

Author/Editor: Rebecca Kerlin
Photography: Ken Yanoviak, Joe Painter, Silicon Graphics, Mia Rosenthal

ISBN-13: 978-1496008916

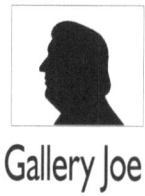

Gallery Joe